DAVID O. MCKAY

D0979287

Group Checkout:
  1 Book
  1 CD

KNOW YOUR BIRD SOUNDS

Volume 2: Songs and Calls of
Birds of the Countryside

WITHDRAWN

MAR 07 2023

DAVID O. McKAY LIBRARY
BYU-IDAHO

MAY 13 2004

0 11557 02964 2

PROPERTY OF:
DAVID O. McKAY LIBRARY
BYU-IDAHO
REXBURG ID 83460-0405

KNOW YOUR BIRD SOUNDS

Volume 2: Songs and Calls of Birds of the Countryside

Lang Elliott

NatureSound Studio

STACKPOLE BOOKS

Copyright © 2004 by Lang Elliott

Published by
STACKPOLE BOOKS
5067 Ritter Road
Mechanicsburg, PA 17055
www.stackpolebooks.com

All rights reserved, including the right to reproduce this book or portions thereof in any form or by any means, electronic or mechanical, including photocopying, recording, or by any information storage and retrieval system, without permission in writing from the publisher. All inquiries should be addressed to Stackpole Books, 5067 Ritter Road, Mechanicsburg, PA 17055.

Printed in China

10 9 8 7 6 5 4 3 2 1

This is a revised and expanded edition of the book originally published in 1991 by NatureSound Studio and in 1994 by NorthWord Press.

Photo Credits: Lang Elliott: cover, 10, 22, 26, 34, 36, 40, 54, 56, 58, 60, 64, 66, 72; Marie Read: 12, 14, 16, 18, 20, 24, 28, 30, 32, 38, 42, 46, 48, 50, 52, 62, 74, 76; TomVezo.com: 44, 68, 70, 78

Library of Congress Cataloging-in-Publication Data

on file with the Library of Congress

Contents

Credits and Acknowledgments vi

Introduction 1
Bird Sound Basics 2
Classification and Functions
   of Bird Sounds 3
The Sound Repertoire 4
More about Bird Song 5
   Special Types of Song 6
   Counter-Singing, Song-
      Matching, and Duetting . . . 7
   Vocal Imitation 7
Remembering Bird Sounds 8

Open Country and Brushy Areas
1. American Goldfinch 10
2. Eastern Meadowlark 12
3. Northern Bobwhite 14
4. Eastern Kingbird 16
5. Killdeer 18
6. Barn Swallow 20
7. Indigo Bunting 22
8. Yellow Warbler 24
9. Eastern Towhee 26

Marsh, Lake, Stream, and Swamp
10. Canada Goose 28
11. Mallard 30
12. Spotted Sandpiper 32
13. Tree Swallow 34
14. Marsh Wren 36

15. Common Yellowthroat 38
16. Red-winged Blackbird 40
17. Barred Owl 42

Forest and Pine Woods
18. Great Horned Owl 44
19. Downy Woodpecker 46
20. Hairy Woodpecker 48
21. Pileated Woodpecker 50
22. Great-crested Flycatcher 52
23. Eastern Wood-Pewee 54
24. Wood Thrush 56
25. Rose-breasted Grosbeak 58
26. Scarlet Tanager 60

Northwoods and High Mountains
27. Yellow-bellied Sapsucker . . . 62
28. Hermit Thrush 64
29. Dark-eyed Junco 66
30. Common Raven 68
31. Common Loon 70

Salt Marsh and Seashore
32. Least Tern 72
33. Herring Gull 74
34. Clapper Rail 76
35. Willet 78

Master List of CD Contents 80

Credits and Acknowledgments

Know Your Bird Sounds, Volume Two was created and produced by Lang Elliott, owner and operator of NatureSound Studio.

The Sound Recordings: The majority of recordings used in this work were collected in the field by Lang Elliott. Additional recordings were supplied by Bill Evans, Ted Mack, Gene Morton, Gary Ritchison, and the Borror Laboratory of Bioacoustics at Ohio State University.

Sources: Information about sound repertoires was gleaned from the extensive scientific literature. Special thanks to Donald and Lillian Stokes for the sound repertoire summaries and bibliographies provided in their *A Guide to Bird Behavior, Volumes 1–3* (Little, Brown). The Stokes' terminology and functional interpretations were followed whenever appropriate.

Review and Criticism: Bill Evans acted as chief consultant for this production. Information about the sound repertoires of select species was provided by Gene Morton (Smithsonian Institution) and Gary Ritchison (Eastern Kentucky University). Although the possibility for errors has been minimized, the author assumes complete responsibility for any identification or classification errors that might become apparent in the future.

Introduction

*I*magine that it is spring. Darkness gives way to dawn, and the landscape brightens with the sounds of countless birds. Nature's melody flows in through open windows, caresses us with a gentle touch, and refreshes our spirits as we awaken to the new day.

Who has not experienced this tonic effect of bird sound? And who is not moved by the sight and sound of colorful birds, perched atop trees and shrubs, singing excited melodies with heads held high and beaks wide open? During all seasons, listening to the sounds of birds is a joyful and uplifting experience, even when one is totally unaware of the identities of the soundmakers involved.

However, an even richer experience awaits those who explore further— those who develop the ability to identify and understand the varied sounds of familiar birds. When such understanding is obtained, each sound will effortlessly bring forth a vibrant image of the soundmaker, even when the soundmaker is not visible. Not only will sounds evoke images, they will betray each bird's behavior. Through sound alone, one will know when territorial encounters are in progress, when courtship is taking place, and when predators are threatening nest or young. Stated simply, bird sound provides an excellent doorway into the intimate, personal lives of the birds that surround you.

This unique audio guide presents the basic sound repertoires of thirty-five common birds found in countryside settings. Over 150 different types of sounds are included, along with information about their meanings. With the help of this guide, you will move quickly ahead with your personal exploration of the exciting world of bird sound and behavior. Wonderful experiences await you!

Bird Sound Basics

Most of the bird sounds that we hear have evolved as communication signals that transfer useful information from one individual to others of the same species. Some sounds, such as the alarm calls made when a bird swoops at a predator, have obvious effects on other species as well. They irritate the predator, and, at the same time, attract other kinds of birds that join in the effort to drive the predator away.

Certain sounds, while bringing attention to a bird, do not function specifically as communication signals. Examples include the subtle noises made by birds as they hop about in leaves or tap at seeds or nuts. Most wing sounds also fit this category.

One may also distinguish between vocal and nonvocal communication signals. In birds, vocal sounds, or vocalizations, are produced by a specialized internal organ called the syrinx, located low in the bird's windpipe where the trachea first branches. As a general rule, those species with the best-developed syrinxes are capable of producing the most complex sounds. Not surprisingly, the birds we call songbirds (also known as passerines, or perching birds) have the most highly developed vocal organs. Nearly all prominent bird sounds that we hear during typical excursions in the outdoors are vocalizations, and the majority are made by songbirds.

Nonvocal sounds can also function as communication signals. Examples include the drumming of woodpeckers, the specialized wing sounds of pigeons and doves in flight, and the bill-snapping of certain owls. Nonvocal signals are most likely to occur among non-songbirds that have poorly developed syrinxes.

Classification and Functions of Bird Sounds

A mong songbirds, a distinction is made between song and calls. Song is usually a complex auditory signal that is musical or "songlike" to our ears. It is typically produced only by males, and only during the spring and early summer breeding season. Especially during the early hours of the morning, males repeat song after song from prominent perches, in the absence of obvious stimuli.

Song has several functions. First and foremost, it is an expression of territory ownership. By singing, resident males alert other males of the same species that their territory is occupied and likely to be defended. Song also helps unmated males attract mates. And, once mating has occurred, song helps maintain pair bonds by assuring a female that her mate is nearby, and that "all is well."

Technically, the term song applies only to songbirds, but many nonpasserines make sounds that have similar functions. Good examples include the yodel of the Common Loon, the hooting of owls, and the drumming of various woodpeckers.

The term "call," when applied to birds, is broad in definition and includes all utterances that cannot be classified as song. Calls are usually simple in structure. Most are given in response to specific stimuli, and calling bouts are normally short-lived. Many calls are produced by both sexes, and by immature as well as mature birds. Furthermore, calls often occur both inside and outside the breeding season. Given their different criteria, it is usually quite easy to distinguish calls from song. Calls have a variety of functions. There are alarm calls; flocking calls; feeding calls; contact calls; begging calls; aggressive, or agonistic, calls; flight calls; and many others. Some are quite specialized in their use and effect. For instance, the twitter call of the Red-winged Blackbird is an intimate vocalization that invites the attention of the mate and often leads to copulation.

While bird song draws our attention because of its musical quality, calls actually reveal more about the intimate lives of birds. They alert us to behavior in progress: territorial squabbles, courtship encounters, predator alarm situations, youngsters demanding food, and the like. Without doubt, recognizing calls and their meanings is a crucial step toward gaining a useful appreciation of the languages of the birds.

In this guide, the functions of calls, when they are known, are described briefly in the audio narrative. More detail can be found in the written species accounts. The functions of song are not discussed for each bird because they are more or less the same for all species. Refer to the information presented above if you forget the basic meanings of song.

The Sound Repertoire

The combination of all auditory signals made by a particular species makes up its sound repertoire. This repertoire provides the basic building blocks for the language of the species. Most birds utilize a fixed number of well-defined vocal or nonvocal signals, which they use separately or in combination to bring about communication. In contrast, some birds utilize signals that lie along a continuum, with one call type grading into another in a continuous and gradual manner.

The exact meanings of specific vocal or nonvocal sounds are often difficult to discern. Identical sounds used in different situations may have different effects, and meanings may vary depending on which sex or age class produces or hears a particular sound. Meanings are inferred by the careful study of context—the participants, actions, and reactions that occur in situations where the auditory signals are used.

Scientific studies show that most species have anywhere from several to twenty or more auditory signals that they use to bring about communication. In this guide, the most important and frequently heard elements of each bird's repertoire are emphasized. Certain rare call types are not included, and nestling sounds have been generally excluded. However, great care has been taken to present an auditory sample that truly reflects each bird's soundmaking ability.

More about Bird Song

O f all the sounds made by songbirds, song attracts the most attention. However, it is interesting to note that certain songbirds lack a clearly defined song. Examples include highly social birds such as the Common Raven and its relative, the American Crow. In these species, males and females look alike, individuals often feed together in groups, and breeding pairs are not clearly territorial. Apparently, song is not necessary to assure breeding success in these species.

The majority of songbirds do sing, but the details of song structure and delivery vary tremendously from species to species. As a rule, the songs of any one species are quite distinct from the songs of other species. These "species-specific" differences allow us humans (and the birds) to confidently use songs as species identifiers, even when singers are not actually seen.

Some species have simple and call-like songs that vary little between individuals. For instance, male Eastern Phoebes (covered in Volume 1) repeatedly sing a buzzy *fee-beee . . . fee-beee . . .* for minutes on end. Phoebe song is very stereotyped, and the songs of different individuals are difficult, if not impossible, to distinguish.

In contrast, certain other species have complex and musical songs that they repeat with only minor variation. The Indigo Bunting is a good example. Each individual sings musical but stereotyped songs that vary only in length. Interestingly, different individuals often have different-sounding songs. Nonetheless, the songs of all males of the species possess a common "bunting quality" that makes them easy to recognize as Indigo Bunting songs, in spite of their variability.

Wood Thrushes show a more complicated pattern. Individuals have a variety of different song patterns in their repertoire. They do not sing these patterns in any specific sequence, but successive songs are usually different. Furthermore, individuals tend to possess a number of unique songs, making it possible for males to actually recognize specific neighbors, based entirely on the individuality of their songs.

Catbirds, mockingbirds, and thrashers (covered in Volume 1) fit yet another category. They sing long, continuous songs made up of a great variety of phrases. Each individual has a vocabulary consisting of a large number of phrase types that it combines in countless ways to produce a song pattern that seems continuously variable and ever-changing.

Clearly, there is considerable variation in the details of singing behavior among songbirds. Each species must be studied carefully before its pattern can be described and understood.

SPECIAL TYPES OF SONG

The typical song of a species may be termed its territorial song. This is the type of song we are most likely to hear during excursions outdoors. However, under certain circumstances birds may sing special songs that sound different from typical song.

For instance, a variety of birds have a dawn song, or twilight song, that they sing during the hour before sunrise. The Eastern Wood-Pewee is a good example. Males sing a distinctive dawn song that sounds noticeably different from their normal song. The primary function of dawn song in pewees and other species is not clearly understood.

Another special song is aggressive song, usually given when an excited male is involved in a territorial encounter. While most birds simply increase the cadence of their singing in such situations, species such as the Yellow Warbler, sing a noticeably different song type that betrays their aggressive mood.

During the height of courtship, a male may approach a female and sing an excited, continuous courtship song that often leads to copulation. Species showing this behavior include several backyard favorites: the House Finch, Purple Finch, and House Wren (covered in Volume 1). The twitter song of the Marsh Wren may also qualify as courtship song.

Yet another special song type is flight song, often given as males flutter slowly upward in what is termed "moth flight." The Indigo Bunting often sings its typical song in flight. In contrast, the Common Yellowthroat sings a unique flight song that is noticeably different from typical song. The dawn song of the Tree Swallow also qualifies as flight song because it is often given by flying birds.

Among temperate zone songbirds, song is usually restricted to males. However, female song occurs in some species. Female Rose-breasted Grosbeaks, Scarlet Tanagers, and Wood Thrushes have been observed singing songs that sound much like those of the males. On the other hand, female

Red-winged Blackbirds have a songlike vocalization that sounds entirely different from the male's song.

COUNTER-SINGING, SONG-MATCHING, AND DUETTING

During territorial encounters, neighboring individuals of a species may sing back and forth in an alternating fashion, a phenomenon known as counter-singing. When such clear alternation is heard, one can be reasonably certain that the birds involved are paying close attention to one another. The Wood Thrush commonly demonstrates counter-singing behavior, and so does the Northern Cardinal.

A related phenomenon is song-matching, often heard among Northern Cardinals and Tufted Titmice (covered in Volume 1). In both species, individuals have repertoires consisting of several different song patterns. During bouts of counter-singing, the participating birds often "match songs" by converging upon the same or similar patterns. Not surprisingly, song-matching and counter-singing often go hand in hand.

In the tropics, a variety of species demonstrate song-duetting, where both members of a pair sing together in a closeknit fashion. Song-duetting is rare among temperate zone birds, but some species show related forms of duetting. For instance, female Red-winged Blackbirds often make a harsh sputtering call just as the male sings. The greeting ceremony of the Great-crested Flycatcher also qualifies as a type of duetting. Duetting helps strengthen pair bonds and may send a strong territorial message to potential intruders.

VOCAL IMITATION

It is well-known that certain species of wild birds imitate the sounds of other species. Usually, they insert imitations into their songs, mixing them with their own sounds. The Northern Mockingbird and European Starling are superb imitators. Catbirds and thrashers (covered in Volume 1) also add imitations to their songs.

The function of vocal imitation remains unclear. However, our native imitators do allow us to test our ability to identify common bird sounds. Listen carefully to the songs of mockingbirds and starlings and see how many imitations you can recognize. The greater your knowledge of bird sounds, the more imitations you will hear!

Remembering Bird Sounds

A useful aid to remembering bird sounds is to fix a name to each sound. In this guide, care has been taken to give each sound a name that accurately describes the sound. A reference list of sound categories is provided at the end of this booklet. After you're somewhat familiar with the bird sounds presented, use the list to test your memory of each bird's repertoire and the names of the various calls.

Some names are onomatopoeic, that is, pronouncing the word or phrase imitates the actual sound. Onomatopoeic memory phrases are a great aid to remembering certain bird sounds. For example, the nonsense phrase *see-ya, see-yer* approximates the slurred tonal changes in the Eastern Meadowlark's song, and the word phrase *drink your tea* informs us of the basic structure of the Eastern Towhee's song. Likewise, words or letter groups like *chip, churr, tsk,* and *bzzz,* when pronounced, actually sound like specific bird calls.

Certain names, such as the "whinny call," of the Downy Woodpecker, liken the actual sound to a reference sound with which we are familiar—in this case, the whinny of a horse. Still other names, such as "whining call" or "whistle call," refer to a well-known category or quality of sound. In some instances, the function of a sound is used to create a name: "alarm *chip*s," "greeting duet," "begging call," and so forth.

Memorizing the names of sounds and associating them with images seen in bird guides is a useful learning technique. But the best learning style of all is to immerse yourself in direct outdoor observation. When you have actually heard sounds in natural settings, and seen the soundmakers in action, the sounds and sights together will make a lasting impression and you will have little trouble remembering them. While this guide can give form and structure to your outdoor explorations, the outdoor experience itself should be your final and ultimate goal. Happy listening!

Sounds of Birds of the Countryside

One of the most common feeder birds across North America, the American Goldfinch male (5 inches long) is easily identified by its lemon yellow color with black wings, cap, and tail. The female is duller and lacks the black cap. Found in open country, goldfinches flock in the spring and often sing in choruses. They nest late, usually in July and August, when they may be seen collecting thistledown for their nests.

Perchickory Flight Call (both sexes): The common flight call of the goldfinch is a melodic, whistled *perchickory* or *perteeteetee*. This distinctive sound is given as birds swing upward during undulating flight motions. Similar calls are made by perched birds.

Su-weeet Call (both sexes): Another common goldfinch call is a nasal *su-weeet*, which probably indicates mild alarm. Breeding birds often make this call near their nest, and it is commonly given by wintering birds as they vie for food at bird feeders.

Song (males only): The song of the male goldfinch is a lively series of high trills, twitters, and whistles, with *su-weeet* calls interspersed. Many of the notes making up song are repeated two or three times. In spring, males sing a long and nearly continuous version of song, and it is common at this time for flocks of males to sing together from treetops and other perches. A short version of their song, lasting two or three seconds, predominates during the summer nesting period.

Bear-bee and Sipperree Calls (both sexes): In situations of extreme alarm, especially near the nest, goldfinches repeat a vibrant *bear-bee . . . bear-bee*. Another alarm note sounds like *sipperree* or *fripperree*.

Chip-pee Call (fledglings only): A staccato *chip-pee, chip-pee*, with the accent on the first syllable, is given by fledglings from late summer to early autumn. This sound is made by perched and flying birds, and seems to act both as a begging call and contact note. The young stop making this call once they are independent of their parents.

2. Eastern Meadowlark

A familiar meadow bird, the Eastern Meadowlark (9¹/₂ inches long) is recognized by its brown back, yellow breast, and the striking black "V" on its chest. Often observed singing from a fence post or telephone line, the meadowlark's whistled *spring-o-the-year* is a fingerprint of open grassland habitat throughout the East, although meadowlarks appear to be declining in some areas. When flushed, its white outer tail feathers are an obvious field mark.

Song (males only): The song of the male consists of a variable number of clear whistles, most being down-slurred. A common four-note pattern sounds like *see-ya, see-yer* or *spring-o-the-year*. Songs may contain up to eight notes or as few as two notes, but most have from three to five. Sometimes the whistles have a burry quality. Meadowlarks occasionally sing in flight.

Chatter Call (both sexes): A harsh chatter is often given during interactions between mates. In early phases of courtship, the female commonly makes this sound when she hears her mate sing.

Dzeet! Call (both sexes): A loud and buzzy *dzeet!* is used in a variety of alarm situations. It may be given in response to predators, but also occurs during territorial encounters and courtship. *Dzeet!*s often precede chatter calls.

Bjeeert Call (both sexes): Another meadowlark call is a buzzy *bjeeert*, more drawn-out and resonant than the similar *dzeet!* call, and usually given by itself. This note probably indicates alarm.

3. Northern Bobwhite

The Northern Bobwhite (9¹/₂ inches long) is the East's only native quail. Its small round body with short tail and neck make it quite distinctive. Hard to spot in thick cover because of their mottled reddish and grayish plumage, bobwhites can be easily located by their distinctive whistled *bob-white!* Outside the breeding season, they cluster in coveys (groups of around twelve birds) and range about on farmland near roadsides, edges, and brushy open areas.

***Bob-white!* Call (males only):** This species gets its name from an easily recognized call of the male: a clear, whistled *bob-white!* At close range, a soft introductory note is often evident: *ah-bob-white!* This songlike utterance is the territorial and breeding call of the male. It is given in spring and early summer as the breeding season unfolds. Neighboring males often alternate calls, much like the counter-singing of certain songbirds.

***Hoy-pei* Separation Call (both sexes):** When individuals are separated from a flock or covey, they respond with a vibrant *hoy* or *hoy-pei*, which they may repeat in a series. This separation call of the bobwhite probably communicates mild alarm coupled with a desire to make contact with other birds. Similar calls are given by covey members at dawn or dusk near roosting sites. During the breeding season, mates use this call to find one another when separated.

***Hoy-poo-weigh* Call (males; sometimes females):** Males involved in territorial disputes and courtship make a call that sounds similar to the separation call, but that is composed of three or more separate syllables: *hoy-poo-weigh* or *hoy-poo-weigh-who*, and the like. Males commonly follow this with their *bob-white!* call, or mix the two: *hoy-poo-bob-white!* Females sometimes give this sound during aggressive interactions.

Alarm Peeps and Whines (both sexes): When young are threatened, adults respond with a variety of high notes, some sounding like the peeping of baby chickens (*peep-peep-peep* . . .) and others having a whining or nasal quality (*psieu-psieu-psieu* . . .).

Intense Alarm Sounds (both sexes): In situations of intense alarm, especially when predators are near, bobwhites make harsh, stuttering sounds and high, wavering squeals. A distinctive stuttering call ends with a long series of rapidly repeated notes: *toil-ick-ick-ick-ick-ick-ick-ick-ick* . . .

The Eastern Kingbird (8 inches long) is commonly seen perched on tree-tops or telephone wires looking for insects, or fluttering in midair to catch its prey. Dark above and light below, kingbirds have a prominent white-tipped tail. The male has a red crown that is hard to see in the field. Kingbirds prefer open spaces and watery areas for hunting, where they search for insects as well as fruits and berries.

***Zeet!* and *K'tsee* Calls (both sexes):** Kingbirds have two common call notes: a harsh, strident *zeet!* and a metallic *k'tsee*. Both calls are given in a variety of situations. The *k'tsee* call is often made by solitary birds, but may also be used during social encounters. The *zeet!* call seems to indicate a high level of arousal. It is often used during aggressive encounters and fights.

***Kitter* Call (both sexes):** When members of a pair or family group come together, they greet one another with a rapid series of high-pitched notes sounding like *kitter-kitter-kitter-kitter* . . . The *kitter* call is usually given in flight as one bird flutters in front of the other.

Dawn Song (males only): Although a songbird, the kingbird lacks a typical song that it repeats throughout most of the day. However, breeding males put on a special performance during the hour before sunrise, and sometimes at dusk. From perches they sing a long and rapid series of strident, high-pitched notes regularly interrupted by loud, buzzy calls: *t-t-t-t-zeet-t-t-t-t-zeet-t-t-t-t-zeet-zeet-t-t-t* . . .

The Killdeer (10 inches long) gets its name from its distinctive call. Brown above and white below with an orange rump, this plover's two prominent black breast bands serve to identify it. Killdeers may nest near water on shores and riverbanks, or far from water in short-grassed fields or pastures. They are well known for a broken wing display, used to lure predators away from their nest.

Killdeer Call (both sexes): Early in the breeding season, individuals of both sexes fly in large circles above their breeding territories, repeating the call that gives rise to their name: *killdeer, killdeer, killdeer* . . . This display may help Killdeers establish territory boundaries. Mates often perform this behavior together.

Deee!, Ki-dee-dee, and Deet Calls (both sexes): Killdeers make a variety of plaintive calls. Simple *deee!* or *deah* notes are often given by foraging birds; they probably indicate mild excitement. An emphatic *ki-dee-dee* or a repeated *deet-deet-deet* . . . is often given in situations of greater alarm. These calls tend to grade into one another, with loudness and repetition rate increasing with alarm. Such calls given near the nest are usually accompanied by a "distraction display," where the parent holds its wings to the side, spreads its tail, and runs about on the ground as if injured.

Flight Alarm (both sexes): When startled into flight, Killdeers make a rapid sputter of short *dee* notes sounding like *dee* . . . *d-d-d-d-d-d-d-d-d* . . . *dee* . . . *dee*. More rarely, flight alarm includes squealing calls that have a metallic, ringing quality.

Stutter Call (both sexes): During a variety of social encounters, and sometimes during alarm, Killdeers make a rapid, stuttering series of high-pitched notes: *t-t-t-t-t-t-t-t-t* . . .

6. Barn Swallow

True to their name, Barn Swallows (7 inches long) build their mud and grass nests in barns and other human-built structures such as bridges, culverts, and garages. These graceful flyers have deeply forked tails, dark blue backs, orange throats, and orange buffy underparts, and skim the ground and water seeking insects. Several pairs may nest in the same area, but they do not form large colonies.

Typical Song (both sexes; mostly males): The song of the Barn Swallow is an excited series of variable, harsh, squeaky notes, interspersed with grating clicks or trills. Males often sing while sitting together on a telephone wire or other perch, but may also sing in flight while chasing females. Females are known to sing, and youngsters begin making song-like sounds within a month of leaving the nest.

Dawn Song (males only): During the hour before sunrise, male Barn Swallows sing a structured version of song that includes repeated elements and periodic sweet notes. Grating clicks are usually absent from dawn song and males generally sing by themselves from a perch.

Chit Call (both sexes): A very common call of the Barn Swallow is a short, staccato *chit*. In alarm situations around the nest, loud *chit*s are given in a rapid series: *chit-chit-chit-chit*. *Chit* calls are also made by flying birds as they forage on the wing.

Cheedeep! Call (both sexes): Another common Barn Swallow call is a ringing, two-parted *cheedeep!* or *beedeep!* This call is often given by flying birds, especially in alarm situations around the nest. *Cheedeep!* probably indicates a high level of arousal.

Nestling Calls (both sexes): When being fed, Barn Swallow nestlings make excited outbursts of harsh, grating notes.

The bright blue male Indigo Bunting ($5^1/_2$ inches long) is a sight to behold, singing from the top of a shrub or flying about in forest clearings, in pastures, and along roadsides. In poor light, the male may appear blackish in color. Females are plain brown and usually remain hidden near their nest in brushy areas. Indigo Buntings are sometimes confused with Eastern Bluebirds, but the latter have rusty red breasts.

Song (males only): The song of the male is a loud series of high-pitched note groups delivered with an even rhythm. Some notes occur only once, but most are given in pairs. The overall structure of a typical song is indicated by the following phrases: *fire-fire, where-where, here-here, see it–see it*, or else *tee, tyu-tyu, chew-chew, tee-tee, seet*. The songs of individual males are rather stereotyped, but males may change song length by adding or deleting note groups. Most songs last from about two to six seconds. Males sometimes sing in flight.

Zeeep Call (both sexes): Indigo Buntings make a high-pitched, buzzy *zeeep* in a variety of circumstances. *Zeeep* calls are often given in flight and may be heard during all seasons, especially in the autumn. They probably function as contact calls.

Chip! Call (both sexes): The alarm call of the bunting is a sharp *chip!* given when nest or young are threatened.

8. Yellow Warbler

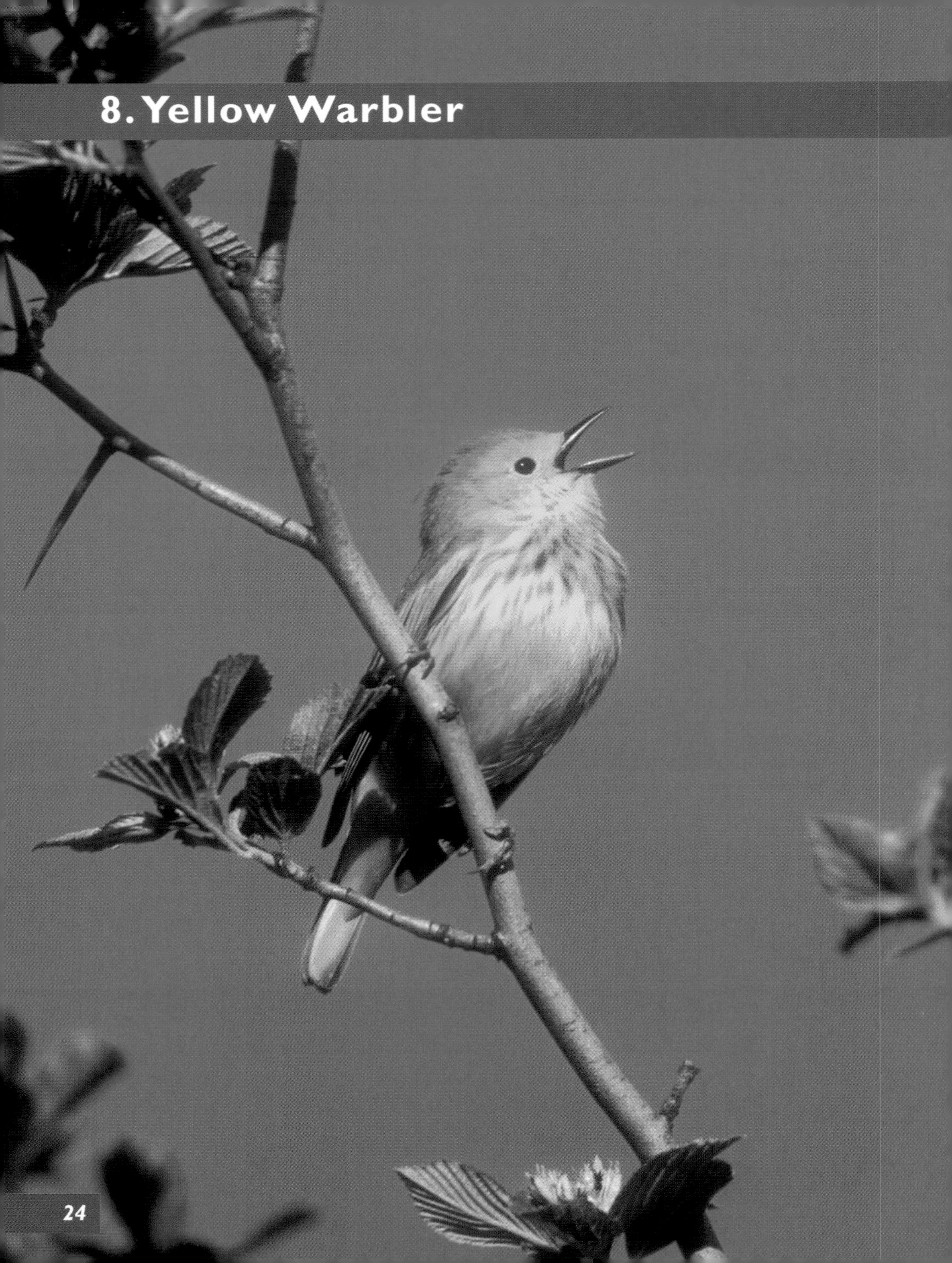

O ne of the most common and easily observed of the wood-warblers, the Yellow Warbler (5 inches long) is bright yellow below and yellow-green above. Males have reddish streaks on their breasts. Yellow Warblers nest in brushy areas and shrub swamps.

Typical Song (males only): The male's bright and cheerful song is a rapid series of high-pitched notes roughly conforming to the pattern *sweet-sweet-sweet-titi-swee!* A common memory phrase is: *sweet-sweet-sweeter-than-sweet!* The last few notes are delivered rapidly with a slight accent at the end. This is the dominant song type given by males as they go about their daily routine.

Encounter Song (males only): During territorial encounters with rivals, males sing a song type that lacks the typical accented ending. Encounter songs usually end with two identical notes: *swee-swee*. A common phrasing sounds like: *sweet-sweet-sweet-swee-swee*. Another sounds like: *sweet-sweet-disee-swee-swee*.

Squeaky *Chip*-Series (males only): During and after intense territorial disputes, males make a long series of squeaky *chip*s that probably reflect their high level of arousal.

Seeet Call (both sexes): The contact call of the Yellow Warbler is a high-pitched and slightly buzzy *seeet*. This call is often given as a bird takes flight. It is often heard late in the season and during migration.

Chip Call (both sexes): The alarm call of the Yellow Warbler is a sharp, high-pitched *chip* or *chewk*.

9. Eastern Towhee

O ften heard scratching noisily on the ground in the brushy areas, the Eastern Towhee (8 inches long) usually stays well-hidden. The male has a black head and black upperparts, a white belly, and rufous-colored sides (hence its former name, Rufous-sided Towhee). The female is brown above. Towhees in the north have red eyes; birds of the far south and Florida have white eyes. Towhees prefer underbrush in open woods and dense edges.

Chuwee Call (both sexes): The most common call of the towhee is a rising *chuwee, tawee*, or *chewink*. This distinctive call is given in a variety of circumstances. It often indicates alarm, but may also be used as a general contact call between mates or family members.

Song (males only): The male's variable song ends with a high trill and usually sounds like the phrase: *drink-your-teeeeee*. Short versions sounding like *your-teeeeee*, or simply *teeeeee*, are common, and more extreme variants also occur. Each male has several different song types in its repertoire and sings one for awhile before switching to another. Males usually sing from perches, but occasionally sing while feeding on the ground.

Disjointed Song and Call–Series (both sexes?): Towhees sometimes make an extended but disjointed series of sounds that include various calls (especially high *chip*s) and song fragments. Usually, the soundmaker is hidden in thick shrubbery. The series is delivered quietly in comparison to song. Its function is not known.

Other Calls (both sexes): During social interactions and at other times, towhees make a variety of calls. One common note is a high-pitched *chip*, perhaps indicating alarm. A quiet call that is easily overlooked is a thin and hissy *seeee*, possibly functioning as a contact call. Towhees also make a nasal *woik-woik-woik*, which seems to communicate aggression and dominance.

The Canada Goose (24 to 45 inches long) is the most familiar goose in North America. Both sexes are brown with black heads and necks and distinctive white chin patches. There is considerable size variation among different populations. Geese from the northern prairie are the largest, with some individuals being nearly four feet long. Canada Geese are strongly monogamous: mates remain paired as long as both live.

Ahonk (both sexes): The most common vocalization of the Canada Goose sounds like *ahonk . . . ahonk*. The female's version is slightly higher in pitch than the male's and sounds more like *ahink*. This is the basic sound made by geese in a variety of situations. It is made by migrating groups as they pass by overhead.

Duetting (performed by mated pairs): Especially when flying, pairs often alternate and overlap their calls in a very precise manner. The resulting duet sounds like *ahink-ahonk-ahink-ahonk . . .* or just *hink-honk-hink-honk-hink-honk . . .* as if one bird were vocalizing.

Hink! Call (females only): In alarm situations, females make a sharp, bark-like *hink!* This call is given when young are threatened, and may also occur during aggressive encounters between pairs.

Hiss Call (both sexes): When extremely alarmed, especially around nest or young, adults make a long and drawn-out hissing sound, *sssssssssssssss*, that is quite unlike any other goose calls. The hiss is usually given with the neck coiled back and the head lowered.

Gosling Sounds (both sexes): While following their parents about, goslings make high, wavering whistles that have an otherworldly quality. The pitch of this call gradually drops as goslings grow older.

Perhaps the most familiar of our native ducks, the Mallard (22 inches long) is a bird of ponds, marshes, streams, and lakes. The colorful male is recognized by his iridescent green head and neck, chestnut breast, and white neck ring. Females are brown and heavily streaked. Both sexes have purple-blue wing patches. A Mallard feeds by dabbling on the surface of the water or by thrusting its head underwater and pointing its tail skyward.

Decrescendo *Quack*-Series (females only): When separated from her mate, the hen Mallard establishes contact with a loud series of about seven or eight *quack*s that decrease in volume and pitch: *qua-QUACK-Quack-quack-quack-quack*. This decrescendo *quack*-series may also be given by unmated females searching for mates.

Persistent *Quack*-Series (females only): In the spring, during the prelaying period when a pair first settles on a breeding area, the flying or swimming female often *quack*s persistently for long periods. The *quack*s are evenly spaced and of constant intensity: *quack, quack, quack, quack, quack, quack* . . . A more excited *quack*-series occurs when alarmed hens take flight.

Female Cackling (females only): During courtship, when hens are approached by males other than their mates, they respond with froglike cackles as they swim after their mate and repeatedly flick their bill to one side of their body: *cack!-cack!-cack!-cack!* . . . This behavior is known as "inciting" because it seems to stimulate the male to action.

***Rhaeb* Call (males only):** Male or drake Mallards do not *quack* like hens. Their common call is a soft, nasal *rhaeb . . . rhaeb . . .* that indicates mild arousal or alarm. A doublet version, *rhaeb-rhaeb*, is often given during aggressive encounters between males.

Grunt-whistle (males only): During the courtship phase, swimming males make a surprising sound thought to function as a courtship call: a high whistle preceded by a soft grunt. The grunt-whistle is given as the male rapidly arches his neck upward, points his bill down, and then suddenly tosses a droplet of water into the air. Groups of courting males often break into grunt-whistles simultaneously.

12. Spotted Sandpiper

A lso called "teeter tail," the Spotted Sandpiper (about 8 inches long) is known for its habit of constantly bobbing its tail up and down. Both sexes are brown above and have white undersides peppered with black spots. In flight, their stiff-looking wings vibrate rapidly in a distinctive manner. Spotted Sandpipers inhabit nearly all freshwater habitats and may be seen feeding and nesting along sandy or pebbly shorelines and beaches.

Weet and Peet-weet Calls (both sexes): Two common calls of the Spotted Sandpiper are a clear, high-pitched *weet* and a two-part *peet-weet*, with the accent on the first syllable. Members of a pair use these calls to stay in contact. *Weet* calls may be slowly repeated in situations of mild alarm.

Peet-a-weet! Call (both sexes): Especially during courtship, sandpipers give a rolling *peet-a-weet! peet-a-weet! peet-a-weet!* with the accent on the last syllable of each phrase. This call is often given in flight, and is thought to function as a courtship call.

Rapid Weet-Series (both sexes): During territorial encounters and situations of extreme alarm, aroused sandpipers produce a rapid volley of excited *weet* notes. This excited series is part of a continuum of *weet* type calls given in alarm situations. Isolated *weet*s indicate mild alarm. Slowly repeated *weet*s mean greater arousal. And a rapid *weet*-series given in flight indicates a high level of alarm.

Squeal Call (both sexes): When nest or young are threatened, parents respond with a distraction display that involves running erratically in the front of the predator, fluttering wings and tail as if injured, and making plaintive, squealing calls.

13. Tree Swallow

An early spring migrant, the Tree Swallow (6 inches long) frequents marshes, beaver ponds, and lakes, as well as open fields and meadows. Males are white below and have glossy black heads and backs that reflect iridescent blue or blue-green. Females are duller in color. Tree Swallows are gregarious and nest in tree cavities near water. During the warmer months, they feed on the wing, catching insects while swooping gracefully over water and fields.

Chideep Call (both sexes): The general alarm or excitement call of the Tree Swallow is a liquid *chideep* or *chidideep*, often given as a rapid series. When a predator approaches the nest, parents excitedly give this call as they fly overhead and dive at the predator. *Chideep*s are also made during courtship as swallows chase one another about.

Buzz Call (both sexes): Another alarm call is a strident buzz, usually given in a rapid series. It often occurs during aggressive encounters, including scuffles between rivals during courtship. The buzz call is almost always accompanied by *chideep*s.

Short Song (males only): Early in the breeding season, the male often sings short songs from perches, especially in the presence of its mate. Short song begins with several thin, melodic whistles, which are then followed by a variable warble of notes. When his mate is present, the male often bows in her direction as he sings.

Dawn Song (males only): At dawn, male Tree Swallows sing a special continuous dawn song, given from perches or while flying in circles overhead. Dawn song involves the rough alternation of two phrase types: *teet, trrit, teet, trrit, teet, teet, trrit, teet* . . . The function of dawn song in Tree Swallows is probably associated with territoriality.

14. Marsh Wren

An energetic little brown bird with a white eyebrow, the Marsh Wren (5 inches long) is found in freshwater and brackish marshes throughout much of North America. It is the only wren likely to inhabit tall cattails and bulrushes. The highly vocal male may have several mates, each occupying a different nest on his territory. Globular nests are made of reeds and cattails and have a side entrance.

Song (males only): The song of the male is a bubbling series of reedy, gurgling notes followed by a loud, rattling trill. Some birds begin their song with a soft buzz. During territorial encounters, rivals may give song after song without pause. The Marsh Wren often sings at night.

Buzz Call (males only?): When agitated, males often make harsh, buzzy notes. This same call sometimes occurs at the beginning of song or between songs.

Chit Call (both sexes): The most common call of the Marsh Wren is a staccato *chit, chit, chit* . . . This call is given in a variety of alarm situations and is often doubled: *chitit*.

Churr Call (both sexes?): During social encounters, and especially territorial disputes, aroused individuals make a rattling *churr-churr-churr* . . . The exact function of this call is not known, but it probably indicates aggression or annoyance.

Twitter Song (males only): When a male actively courts a female, he follows her about and makes continuous twittering notes. This song may help secure the pair bond and entice the female to copulate. Excited males may also intersperse twittering notes with typical songs.

15. Common Yellowthroat

The Common Yellowthroat (5 inches long) is a widespread species that frequents moist, shrubby thickets and wet grassy areas with tall bushes. Members of the wood-warbler group, yellowthroats skulk about in thickets looking for insect food. The male is recognized by his bright yellow throat and black mask; the pale female lacks the mask but has a yellow throat.

Song (males only): The bright song of the yellowthroat consists of several identical, high-pitched phrases that are rapidly repeated. Many songs sound similar to *witchity, witchity, witchity* or *wititee, wititee, wititee*, but a variety of phrase patterns and accent variations exist. The songs of individuals are stereotyped, but vary in length.

Flight Song (male only): The male Common Yellowthroat occasionally sings a special flight song, which sounds different from normal song. The performance begins as the male rises into the air over his territory and flies slowly with wings fluttering like a moth. While fluttering, he gives a series of soft, high *tink*s followed by two loud *chip*s. Some typical song phrases follow (*witchity, witchity*) and the performance finally terminates with a garbled group of buzzy notes, given as the yellowthroat flies toward a perch. The function of the male yellowthroat's flight song is not known.

Tschat **and** ***Steek!*** **Calls (both sexes):** The most common alarm call of the yellowthroat is a sharp *tschat* given in response to nearly all disturbances within the territory. In situations of intense alarm, *tschat* calls are accompanied by higher *steek!* calls.

Rapid Chatter (both sexes?): A high-pitched, rapid chatter is commonly given during territorial boundary disputes. The female may use this call to get the attention of her mate. Rapid chatter probably communicates aggressive intent or alarm.

*T*he Red-winged Blackbird (8 inches long) is a common bird of fresh-water and saltwater marshes. The male is jet black with bright scarlet shoulder patches edged in yellow. The female is heavily streaked with dark brown. Although primarily marsh birds, Red-wings also breed in upland pastures, usually near water. Males are often polygamous.

Song (males only): The variable song of the male is a raucous, gurgling *o-ka-leee* or *conk-la-reee*, with almost all songs ending with a buzzy trill. When singing, the male leans forward, cocks his wings, and exposes his red shoulder patches, a display known as a songspread. Each individual has a repertoire of several different song patterns and usually sings a few songs of one pattern before switching to another.

Female Sputter (females only): Red-wing males often have more than one mate, and females within a male's territory actively defend the area around their nest from neighboring females. A common sound made by females in their breeding territories is a rapid sputter of sharp, high-pitched notes, often followed by drawn-out, buzzy sounds. The sputter is given in a variety of situations, and seems to be an aggressive and ter-ritorial display of the female. Some call this vocalization "female song."

Duetting (both sexes together): Throughout the breeding season, a female often gives the sputter call just as her mate sings. This duetting behavior may help establish and maintain pair bonds.

***Tsk!* Call (both sexes):** The most common call of the Red-wing is a harsh, staccato *tsk!* or *check!* This variable call functions as a general contact note, but it may also indicate alarm.

***Seeeyer* Call (males only):** In situations of extreme alarm, such as when a predator enters the nesting territory, males respond with plaintive, down-slurred whistles sounding like *seeeyer* or *seeyeet*. In some regions, the alarm whistles of the males have a burry quality. Neighboring Red-wings become attentive when they hear this call.

Twitter Call (both sexes): During courtship and just prior to copulation, the male and/or female makes a rapid series of high, wavering whistles that have a whimpering quality. This "twitter call" may follow male song or female sputters, and is normally given only when mates are in close proximity to one another.

O ne of our most vocal owls, the Barred Owl (20 inches long) is large and chunky, with a rounded head, dark eyes, and a brown-streaked breast. Barred Owls prefer thick forests and are common residents of wooded swamps. They nest in tree hollows and feed on rodents, frogs, and crayfish. Though primarily nocturnal, Barred Owls often remain active during the day.

Typical Hoot-Series (both sexes): The most well-known call of the Barred Owl is a series of eight hoots likened to the phrase *who cooks for you, who cooks for y'all*. The "southern drawl" at the end may be absent in some birds. The typical hoot series occurs throughout the year and probably acts as a territorial call as well as a long-distance contact call used by mates or family members.

***Whoo-ah* (both sexes):** Another distinctive Barred Owl vocalization is a descending *whoo-ah*, repeated once every minute or so. Individuals sometimes answer one another with this call. The function of the *whoo-ah* call is not known.

Ascending Hoot-Series (both sexes): Barred Owls sometimes produce a series of six or more hoots that ascend in pitch and then end with a down-slurred note. As with most Barred Owl calls, the exact significance of the ascending hoot-series is not known.

Greeting Displays (both sexes): When mates or members of a family group come together after being separated, they often greet one another by overlapping ascending hoots and making excited, monkeylike cries—an outstanding auditory performance that may involve several individuals. Another type of greeting display is a duet where participants overlap laughlike hoots in a rhythmical, structured manner. One senses a joyful reunion when witnessing these displays.

Immature Screech (both sexes): Immature Barred Owls make harsh, screeching sounds that are quite unlike the hoots of adults. These probably function as contact calls and begging calls. Adults are thought to make similar screeching or wailing sounds.

18. Great Horned Owl

The Great Horned Owl (22 inches long) is a stunning bird, not only because of its large size, but also because of its catlike appearance (due to its conspicuous ear tufts). Horned owls are brown or reddish-brown, heavily barred beneath, and have a white throat patch. They are found in a variety of habitats across North America, including swamps, deserts, forests, and even cities. Prey range in size from tiny mice to larger mammals such as skunks or house cats.

Typical Hoot-Series (both sexes): The typical hoot-series of the Great Horned Owl consists of four or five deep, resonant hoots, all given at the same pitch. The rhythm of the hoots is uneven and varies from individual to individual. The hoot-series can be heard year round, but there is a peak of calling in the autumn and winter when pairing occurs. The two sexes often hoot back and forth; the female's hoots are shorter and higher in pitch than the male's.

Barklike Hoots (both sexes): When nest or young are threatened, adults respond with sharp, barklike hoots, given singly.

Screech Calls and Bill-Snapping (mostly immatures): Immatures make a variety of unusual screechlike calls, ranging from high, whistling screeches, to low, growling versions. The exact functions of these calls are not known, although they are generally assumed to be begging calls. Immatures and adults alike snap their bills in protest when alarmed or threatened.

A favorite year-round visitor to bird feeders across the continent is the Downy Woodpecker (7 inches long), our smallest native woodpecker. The black-and-white bird can be recognized by its small size, short bill (about half as long as its head), and its white back. The male has a small red patch on the back of his head. Like other woodpeckers, Downy Woodpecker excavate holes in tree limbs for their nests, especially in dead trees.

***Pik* Call (both sexes):** The most common call of the species is a sharp, dry *pik*, given in a variety of situations. The *pik* call functions both as a contact note and an alarm call.

***Pik*-Series and Subtle *Churr* (both sexes):** When excited, especially during social interactions, Downy Woodpeckers sometimes deliver about five *pik* calls in a short series, the last being emphasized: *pik-pik-pik-pik-peek!* Soft, rattling *churr* calls are also given during interactions.

Whinny Call (both sexes): A distinctive call is a rapid outburst of staccato notes that speed up and then drop in pitch at the end, reminding some of the whinny of a tiny horse. This call is given during aggressive encounters, but also functions as a general contact call.

Harsh Chatter (both sexes?): One uncommon call is a harsh, wrenlike chatter. This call accompanies territorial disputes and other aggressive encounters.

Drumming (both sexes): Both sexes pound their beaks against resonant wood to make a rapid drumming sound. The drumming has an even tempo and lasts about one second. Drumming functions to advertise territory and attract a mate.

Very similar in appearance to the Downy Woodpecker, the Hairy Woodpecker is larger in size (9 inches long) and has a longer bill (about the same length as its head). The male has a red patch on the back of his head. Hairies are year-round residents in woodlands across North America. Although less common than Downy Woodpeckers, they often visit bird feeders and may show up in suburbs or city parks.

Peek Call (both sexes): The most common call of the Hairy Woodpecker is an emphatic *peek*, very similar to the Downy's *pik*, but slightly sharper (one can learn the difference with practice). This call is given year-round, in a variety of situations.

Sputter Call (both sexes): Hairies sometimes produce a rapid sputter of loud *peek* notes. This call sounds similar to the whinny call of the Downy Woodpecker, but has an even tempo and does not drop in pitch at the end. Single *peek* calls usually precede sputters, which are thought to be an expression of territoriality.

Weeka-weeka and Tew-tew Calls (both sexes): During social interactions, and especially courtship encounters, individuals make two types of intimate calls. One is an excited *weeka-weeka-weeka* . . . that is accompanied by waving of the bill. The other is a repeated series of soft *tew* calls, often given when members of a pair rejoin after being separated: *tew-tew-tew-tew-tew* . . .

Drumming (both sexes): The drum of the Hairy Woodpecker is rapid and has an even tempo. Most drums are faster and slightly longer than Downy Woodpecker drums. Drumming probably functions as a territorial and courtship display.

O ur largest and most striking woodpecker, the Pileated Woodpecker (18 inches long) has a flaming red crest and a long pointed beak that allows it to penetrate deep into rotten wood to capture carpenter ants and other insects. The male also has a red line extending off the base of his bill. A denizen of mature forests, these woodpeckers leave characteristic rectangular feeding holes in dead or dying trees. Territories are defended with loud resonant drumming and ringing, laughlike calls.

Short Call (both sexes): A distinctive call of the Pileated Woodpecker is a rapid series of about seven or eight loud and penetrating notes, with the last note often dropping slightly in pitch: *hee-hee-hee-hee-hee-hee-hay!* This long-carrying call helps members of a pair stay in contact, and may also indicate alarm. The short call is often given by birds just before they enter their roost hole at dusk, or upon leaving the hole at dawn, perhaps to alert mates to their whereabouts.

***Cak*-Series (both sexes):** Another call is a slow-paced series of *cak* notes varying in loudness and pace of delivery: *cak-cak-cak-cak-cak-cak* . . . The *cak*-series may last from several seconds to over a minute. This call is given in a variety of situations, often in response to predators or other sources of alarm. It may also act as a general contact call between members of a pair.

***Gawaik-gawaik* (both sexes):** An unusual call sounding like *gawaik-gawaik-gawaik* . . . is given during close range interactions involving courtship or territorial defense. This intimate call is usually accompanied by bill-waving and other physical posturing.

Drumming (both sexes): The drum of the Pileated Woodpecker lasts about two seconds and grows softer right at the end. Due to the large size of this woodpecker, drums are usually louder and more resonant than the drums of smaller woodpecker species. Drumming helps individuals establish territory and attract mates.

A fairly common flycatcher of open woodlands, the Great-crested Flycatcher (8½ inches long) is known for its noisy outbursts of call notes, often given by both members of a pair. Olive brown above, the flycatcher has a gray breast, a yellow belly, and cinnamon-colored wings and tail. Though not always held erect, the bushy crest is often evident. A hole nester, the Great-crested Flycatcher often adds pieces of shed snakeskin to its nest.

Weeeps, Prrrrrt!s, and Outbursts (both sexes): The two most common calls of this flycatcher are a whistled *weeep* or *weeeup*, and a rolling, throaty *prrrrrt!* These calls may be given singly, or combined to produce variable outbursts of loud notes. *Prrrrrt!* calls are often delivered in a rapid series. The functions of these and similar calls are not known, but they are probably used as contact and alarm calls, and may function to establish territories.

Greeting Duets (both sexes together): When members of a pair come together after being separated, they sometimes join together in an excited outburst of loud calls. In many instances, a clear alternation of calls of the two individuals is evident. Even when separated, pairs may answer one another's calls, and even match call types.

Dawn Song (males only): This species does not have a typical daytime song like most songbirds. However, males do sing a special dawn song during the hour before sunrise. Dawn song consists of the alternation of two distinctive kinds of loud whistled phrases that are separated by soft, throaty sounds: *weeyup . . . prr-prr . . . weeyerrr . . . prr-prr . . . weeyup . . . prr . . . weeyerrr . . .*

23. Eastern Wood-Pewee

*T*he Eastern Wood-Pewee (6 inches long) is a small olive-gray flycatcher of eastern deciduous forests that makes its presence known with its plaintive whistled song: *peee-a-wee* or *peeee-oh*. Follow the song and you may find the singer perched on a midstory limb, waiting patiently to snatch an insect in midair. Wood-pewees sing a special twilight song at dawn and then again at dusk.

Normal Song (males only): The plaintive, leisurely song of the male consists of two kinds of slurred, whistled phrases. One phrase sounds like *peee-a-wee*, and the other is a down-slurred *peeee-oh*. These two phrases are roughly alternated and separated by long pauses. Unlike many other songbirds, male pewees sing throughout the day and may be heard from spring until they migrate in early autumn. Note: the *turree* call, described below, may actually be a type of song.

Dawn Song (males only): During the hour before sunrise, pewees sing an excited dawn song made up of three different phrase types separated by short pauses: *peee-a-wee . . . ah-didee . . . peeee-oh . . .* The rising *ah-didee* phrase is peculiar to dawn song. The function of this auditory display is not known.

***Turree* Call (males only):** In late summer, males often make a rising, slurred whistle sounding like *turree*. This call is easily mistaken for the *peee-a-wee* phrase of song, but lacks the middle note. The function of this call is not known, although it is repeated from perches much like song and might be a form of song.

Whines and Sputters (both sexes): During social interactions, pewees make delicate whining or twittering whistles. Such sounds are given by courting pairs, and also by members of a family group. Another intimate encounter call is a loud sputter of harsh notes, possibly indicating aggression.

24. Wood Thrush

The least shy of our native thrushes, the Wood Thrush (8 inches long) frequents suburban woodlots and parklands as well as the deep forest of remote wild areas. It is recognized by its rusty head and back, brown rump and tail, and extensive spotting below. The Wood Thrush is best known for its melodious flutelike song, which has inspired poets and nature writers alike. Wood Thrushes have undergone population declines in many areas in recent years.

Song (males; rarely females): The song of the Wood Thrush is beautiful and flutelike. It begins with one to several soft *tut* notes, which lead into variable melodic phrases that usually terminate with a high, buzzy trill. Common song patterns sound like *tutut-eee-o-lay-o-eeee* or *tutut-eee-ay-eeee*. Each bird has several different song patterns that are not sung in a fixed sequence, although successive songs are usually different. Females sing partial songs during territorial encounters.

***Wit* Volley (both sexes):** During aggressive encounters and other alarm situations, Wood Thrushes respond with excited volleys of variable numbers of sharp and liquid *wit* notes: *wit-wit-wit-wit-wit*. This call may integrate with *bub-bub-bub* calls.

***Bub-bub-bub* Call (both sexes):** An intimate call of the Wood Thrush is a short, rapid volley of soft notes sounding like *bub-bub-bub-bub* . . . Soft *bub* volleys are often alternated with loud *wit* volleys and the two calls may integrate. *Bub*s are used as contact calls between mates and may indicate mild alarm.

***Zeee!* Call (both sexes):** Another Wood Thrush contact call is a buzzy *zeee!* that is usually given singly. This call is made by perched and flying birds. It is commonly given at night by migrating birds flying overhead.

A strikingly colored bird, the male Rose-breasted Grosbeak (8 inches long) is black above, white below, and has a triangle of bright rose-red on the breast. The female is brown above with a streaked breast. In flight, a pattern of white is visible across the back of the male's upper plumage. Rose-breasted Grosbeaks have a beautiful caroling song which has been described as "like a robin who took singing lessons."

Song (both sexes): The grosbeak's song is a melodious series of wavering whistles, similar in quality to the robin's song, but with sweet phrases slurred together and delivered quickly. Females sing on occasion, especially when near their nest.

***Chink* Call (both sexes):** The most common call of the Rose-breasted Grosbeak is a sharp, metallic *chink*, given singly. Soft versions of this note function as contact calls, and louder *chink*s, slowly repeated, indicate alarm. *Chink* calls are often interspersed between songs.

***Teeyoo* Call (fledglings):** Fledgling grosbeaks bring attention to themselves with a burry, down-slurred whistle: *teeyoo*. Fledglings also make *chink* calls and *veee* calls.

***Veee* Call (both sexes):** An intimate contact note of the grosbeak is a buzzy, nasal *veee* or *weee*, usually given singly. This expressive call ranges from soft and melodic to harsh and emphatic. *Veee* calls are commonly given as birds move about in family groups in late summer. Similar calls are made by flying birds.

A flaming torch of red, the Scarlet Tanager (7 inches long), is a treetop bird of mature deciduous forests, especially oak woods. Males are bright scarlet with black wings and tail. Females are a dull yellow-green. More often heard than seen, Scarlet Tanagers are easy to locate by their unique *chick-bree* call and burry robinlike song. Look for the singing male high in the treetops. In the spring, a late freeze will sometimes force tanagers out of the trees to search for insects along roadsides.

Song (males; rarely females): The song of the Scarlet Tanager is a series of hoarse, burry whistles, slurred together and delivered rather quickly. Some liken the song to the imagined sound made by a robin hoarse with a cold. Females occasionally sing.

Chick-bree Call (both sexes): A common call of the Scarlet Tanager is a two-part *chick-bree*. This call is given in situations of alarm, but may also be made in early morning or late evening in the absence of any obvious disturbance. *Chick-bree* calls, and sometimes simple *chick* notes, may be interspersed between songs.

Chip Call (both sexes): In alarm situations, tanagers often respond with loud *chip* calls that are similar in quality to the first note of the *chick-bree* call.

Sweet Call (both sexes?): An intimate call of the Scarlet Tanager is a soft, melodic whistle sounding like *sweet*. The *sweet* call seems to be a contact call used primarily by mates; it can only be heard from several yards away.

The Yellow-bellied Sapsucker ($8^1/_2$ inches long) drills rows of holes in birches, maples, and other trees to produce wells of sap on which it feeds. Sapsuckers are black and white above, with yellowish bellies and red foreheads. The male has a red throat. The common call is a nasal catlike *mew*. Sapsuckers are the only woodpecker in the East with an irregular staccato drumming.

Drumming (both sexes): The drumming display of the sapsucker is easy to distinguish from that of other woodpeckers. It starts with several rapid beats, then slows down to a fairly even tempo with rapid doublets or triplets thrown in: *tutututump-tump-tump-tutump-tutump-tump-tump* . . . Sapsuckers will beat on signs and other resonant, manmade objects. Drumming functions primarily as a territorial and breeding display.

Mew Call (both sexes): Sapsuckers make a variety of mewing sounds or squeals. These are given in times of alarm, and may act as contact notes. Soft versions are often given as birds enter or leave their nest hole.

Squeal-Series (both sexes?): A distinctive sapsucker vocalization is a repeated series of hawklike squealing sounds. This long-carrying call may function as a territorial courtship display.

Grinding Call and Harsh Chatter (both sexes): During social interactions, including aggressive encounters and courtship, aroused sapsuckers make harsh grinding sounds sounding like *skreeek-skreeek-skreeek-skreeek* . . . They repeat this excitedly while bobbing their heads from side to side. Another interaction call is a harsh, rattling chatter, given by birds as they fly from their perch.

28. Hermit Thrush

*P*ossessing a magical, ethereal song, the Hermit Thrush (7 inches long) breeds in coniferous and mixed woodlands of northern or mountainous areas. Identified by its dull brown back, reddish tail, and spotted breast, the Hermit Thrush is the only one of our spotted thrushes to habitually pump its tail up and down. Its beautiful song, which begins with a clear whistle followed by bell-like tones, was aptly described in a poem by John Burroughs: "Oh, holy, holy!"

Song (males only): The beautiful, flutelike song of the male begins with a long, clear whistled note that is steady in tone. This note is followed by a rapid series of rambling, ethereal notes that vary greatly in pitch. Males often sing at dusk.

***Churt* Call (both sexes):** The alarm call of the species is an emphatic *churt*, which is often repeated slowly.

***Wayyy* Call (both sexes?):** Another distinctive Hermit Thrush call is a drawn-out, nasal *wayyy* or *whyyy*. The function of this call is not known. It is often given by solitary birds, and is commonly heard at dusk.

***Veee* Call (both sexes):** The contact call of the species is a loud, whistled *veee*, given by perched or flying birds. *Veee* calls are often made by migrating Hermit Thrushes flying in the night sky.

29. Dark-eyed Junco

A northern or mountain breeding species, the Dark-eyed Junco (6 inches long) is a common snowbird in many regions, showing up at feeders only during the winter months. In the East, juncos are easily identified. Males are slate-gray with a white belly and white outer tail feathers. Females are brownish gray. In the West, juncos come in a variety of color patterns once thought to signify separate species. The musical ringing song of the junco reminds many of the ringing tone of a modern cell phone.

Song (males only): The song of the male is a high-pitched, musical trill lasting about one or two seconds. The songs of different birds often differ in character. Some stay on one pitch while others vary up or down. Some have a slow tempo, with notes almost slow enough to count; others have such rapid note delivery that they may be mistaken for the buzzy trill of an insect.

***Tsip* Call (both sexes):** The contact note of the junco is a high-pitched *tsip*. Individuals of a pair, family group, or winter flock often make this call as they move about together. *Tsip* calls are often given by flying birds.

***Tick* Call (both sexes):** In a variety of alarm situations, juncos respond with a sharp *tick* call. The *tick* alarm note is easy to distinguish from the more delicate *tsip* call.

***Zeeet* and *Titit!* Calls (both sexes):** During aggressive encounters, juncos make buzzy *zeeets*, which appear to convey on aggressive mood. *Zeeets* are often given as a bird lands near a food source, even when other birds are not visible. Another call that occurs during aggressive encounters is a loud, two-part call that sounds like *titit!* It generally indicates a high level of arousal.

Fledgling *Zeeet* Call (both sexes): A call very similar to the adult *zeeet* is given by immatures as they beg for food or attention. These calls are often excitedly repeated by the fledglings.

***Tew-tew* Call (both sexes):** Another junco call that communicates aggressive intentions is a rather musical *tew-tew-tew-tew* . . . that is usually given in a series. This pleasing call is commonly heard outside the breeding season when juncos move about in flocks.

H awklike in appearance, the all-black Common Raven (25 inches long) is much larger than the American Crow and can be distinguished from the latter by its deep croaking voice, its heavier bill, and its shaggy neck feathers. Once rare in the East and confined to remote mountainous areas, the raven is rapidly expanding its range. Like hawks, ravens alternately flap their wings and soar high in the air.

Typical Croaks (both sexes): The most common call type of the raven is a throaty *crrrawk*. This basic sound is given in a variety of situations and often indicates alarm. Croaks are subject to much variation. They range from light and laughlike to loud, boisterous, and assertive. Ravens seem to adapt their croaks to suit their moods.

Immature Harsh Croak (immatures of both sexes; sometimes adult females): The croaks of immature ravens are much harsher than those of adults. Harsh croaks function as begging calls and also serve to appease adults by identifying immatures as nonbreeding birds. Fledglings give excited harsh calls when a parent approaches them for feeding. Adult females give a similar sound when accepting food from their mates.

Low *Crok* (both sexes): When parents approach nest or young with food, they give a very low-pitched *crok*, which is not as harsh and throaty as typical croaks.

Other Raven Sounds (both sexes): Ravens make a great variety of unusual sounds, some sounding quite different from typical croaks. Examples include a hollow *pop-pop-pop*, a gooselike *k'onk . . . k'onk*, a resonant *kowp . . . kowp*, and a very odd *doo-waaaa, doo-waaaa*. The functions of these and related calls are not known, but they attest to the raven's remarkable vocal versatility.

31. Common Loon

The eerie cry of the Common Loon (32 inches long) echoing across a lake is to many symbolic of the northern wilderness. Loons are large, ducklike birds with long pointed beaks, black heads, checkered backs, and white breasts. In summer on their breeding grounds they produce a variety of splendid calls, including wails, tremolos, yodels, and hoots. During courtship, mates race side by side across the surface of the water.

Tremolo Call (both sexes): The alarm call of the Common Loon is a tremulous vibrato of about a second's duration that reminds some of a quavering, maniacal laugh; it is usually repeated in a series. Tremolo calls are given by swimming and flying loons. Excited birds repeat one tremolo after the other and often vary the pitch within each call.

Tremolo Duet (both members of a pair): Members of a pair sometimes alternate and overlap their excited tremolos to produce an impressive duet. Tremolo duets are given in alarm situations, but also may function as territorial displays of the pair.

Wail Call (both sexes): The long-distance contact call of the loon is a wailing sound reminiscent of the howling of a wolf or coyote. Wails last about two seconds and consist of several notes given in succession that usually rise in pitch. Females often wail when their mates yodel.

Yodel Call (males only): The most complex loon vocalization is the male's territorial call, the yodel. Yodel calls start out sounding like wails, but then end with wildly undulating phrases that last several seconds. Yodeling occurs mostly in spring and early summer when males are establishing their breeding territories.

Hoots (both sexes): The most intimate note of the loon is a soft hoot, given by members of a pair, family group, or flocks. Unlike other loon calls, hoots can only be heard at close range.

O ur smallest tern, the Least Tern (9 inches long) is recognized by its yellow bill, black cap, white forehead, gray back, and white under-parts. It nests on islands or isolated beaches where it lays its eggs in a small unlined scrape. Least Terns catch small fish or crustaceans by flying low over the surface of the water and then hovering or suddenly diving for prey.

***Chiddit* Call (both sexes):** The common flight call of the least tern sounds like *chiddit* or *kiddit*. This call often has a ringing, metallic quality. It probably functions as a general contact note or flocking call.

***Chiddy-what-it* Call (both sexes?):** When returning to the nest with a cap-tured fish (to feed mate or young), a flying tern excitedly repeats a com-plex and distinctive vocalization: *chiddy-what-it, chiddy-what-it, chiddy-what-it . . .*

***Chit* Call (both sexes):** In situations of mild alarm, Least Terns make emphatic *chit* calls while flying overhead.

***Zhreeek* Call (both sexes):** In situations of intense alarm, such as when a predator enters the nesting colony, harsh, squealing *zhreeek* calls are given by excited birds flying in circles overhead. Quite often, vocalizing birds dive at the predator, making a loud *zhreeek* at the bottom of each dive.

***Klee*-Series (both sexes):** When a Least Tern flies to its nest, it often makes a rapid series of high, metallic notes: *klee-klee-klee-klee-klee . . .* These notes usually grade into the more typical *chiddit* call. Upon landing, the mates usually switch places at the nest.

33. Herring Gull

The familiar Herring Gull (25 inches long) is named after the fish, which is only part of its highly varied diet. Herring Gulls are common and widespread, especially along the East coast. A large gull, it is recognized by its gray back and upper wings, black wing tips, and white head, tail, and underparts. The bill is yellow with a red spot near the lower tip. Herring Gulls are omnivorous, eating fish and crustaceans, and also scavenging on refuse at dumps.

Klee-ew Call (both sexes): The most common call of the Herring Gull is a loud *klee-ew* or *kleew*. This call is given in a variety of situations during all seasons. *Klee-ew* is contagious—when one bird calls, others do the same. The call's function is not clear, but many consider it a contact call. Loud versions are given when gulls dive at predators.

Mew Call (both sexes): The *mew* call is a drawn-out note with a wailing and plaintive character reminding many of a human voice. The *mew* call indicates breeding activity and a friendly attitude toward mate, territory, nest and young. It is usually given with neck stretched forward and downward and bill opened wide.

Trumpeting Call (both sexes): The most elaborate call of the Herring Gull is the trumpeting call. Trumpeting begins with several low calls and subdued high notes given with head stretched forward then down. Next, the head is thrown upward with a jerk, and a series of loud screams issue forth, given with neck stretched forward and mouth open. The body shakes all over with each scream. The trumpeting call is associated with breeding activity. Mates often perform it as a duet and individuals in groups often trumpet one after the other in close succession.

Ga-ga-ga-ga Call (both sexes): The alarm call of the species is a hoarse, rhythmic *ga-ga-ga-ga*, normally given in flight. Birds making this call are usually on or near the breeding area.

Hough-hough Call (both sexes): When members of a pair make a nest-scrape together, they make an odd, rhythmical series of muted notes as they tip forward, peck at the ground, and scrape the earth with their feet: *hough-hough-hough-hough* . . . Some refer to this sound as the "choking call" because the soundmakers look like they're choking. A similar call may be given during aggressive encounters.

A chickenlike bird of salt marshes along the Atlantic and Gulf coasts, the Clapper Rail (15 inches long) is usually hidden in dense vegetation, but betrays its presence with its staccato clattering calls. The Clapper Rail is brownish in color and has barred flanks and a blackish head. Also called "marsh hens," individuals are sometimes seen in the open, walking along the muddy edges of marshes.

***Kuk-kuk-kuk* Call (both sexes):** The Clapper Rail's most common call is a dry, clattering *kuk-kuk-kuk-kuk* . . . given in a series of variable length and tempo, often speeding up then slowing down. This contagious call is most commonly heard at dusk or on moonlit nights, when salt marshes often come alive with clattering. It probably functions as a contact call and a territorial display.

Grunt-Series (both sexes): During the breeding season, clappers sometimes produce a rapid series of grunting notes that start out fast and then drop in tempo and pitch toward the end. Quite often, mates give this call in unison. The grunt series is contagious; a wave of these calls can pass over a marsh as pair after pair break into the display. This vocalization is thought to be an expression of territoriality.

***Kicker* Call (both sexes?):** Another vocalization attributed to Clapper Rails is called the *kicker* call: *kick-kick-kick-kickerrrrr*. The *kicker* call is usually heard at night and may be given by flying birds. Its function is not known.

*T*he Willet (15^{1}/$_{2}$ inches long) is a large, plain-brown shorebird restricted to coastal areas in the East. When Willets take flight, one is surprised to see a striking black and white wing pattern not visible in the standing bird. Willets are named for their musical call, *willillet*. They nest in colonies in salt marshes, but are often seen feeding along sandy beaches.

Day, Day-dee, and Related Calls (both sexes): A common call of the Willet is a resonant *day* or *day-dee*. Variations on this theme include *day-deeyut* and *day-dee-dee*. These calls may function as contact calls, but also seem to indicate mild alarm. They are given during all seasons, usually by foraging birds.

Willillet Call (both sexes): When startled into flight, alarmed birds respond with series of excited, wavering calls sounding like *willillet* or *willillillet*.

Kip and Keeer Calls (both sexes): Alarm calls given by Willets near the nest include a sharp, metallic *kip* or *kitip* and a harsh, drawn-out *keeer*. These loud calls are made by perched or flying birds when predators threaten nest or young.

Pill-will-willet Call (both sexes): The breeding display of the Willet is a melodic *pill-will-willet, pill-will-willet, pill-will-willet . . .* given by birds as they fly in large circles over their breeding territories.

Master List of CD Contents

Species numbers are equivalent to track numbers on the compact disc. Each species is identified by name and number on the compact disc before its sound repertoire is presented. Written descriptions of each bird's repertoire can be located with ease within this book by referring to the appropriate species numbers as listed below or as heard on the disc.

OPEN COUNTRY AND BRUSHY AREAS

1. American Goldfinch
Perchickory flight call
Su-weeet call
Short song
Group song
Bear-bee and *sipperree* alarm
Chip-pee fledging call

2. Eastern Meadowlark
Song
Chatter call
Dzeet! call
Bjeeert call

3. Northern Bobwhite
Bob-white call
Hoy-pei separation call
Hoy-poo-weigh
Alarm peeps and whines
Squeals and *toil-ick-ick-ick-ick*

4. Eastern Kingbird
Zeet! and *k'tsee* calls
Kitter call (greeting display)
Dawn song
Various calls heard when parent
  feeds fledgling

5. Killdeer
Killdeer call
Deee! or *deeeah* calls
Ki-dee-dee and *deet-deet*
Flight alarm
Stutter call

6. Barn Swallow
Typical song
Dawn song
Chit call
Cheedeep! call
Nestling calls

7. Indigo Bunting
Song
Zeeep call
Chip! call

8. Yellow Warbler
Typical song
Encounter song
Squeaky *chip*-series
Seeet call
Chip alarm

9. Eastern Towhee
Chuwee call
Song
Disjointed song and calls
Seee, chip, and *woik-woik-woik* calls

MARSH, LAKE, STREAM, AND SWAMP

10. Canada Goose
Migrating group calling
Ahonk call
Duetting
Female *hink!* alarm
Hiss alarm
Gosling sounds

11. Mallard
Decrescendo *quack*-series
Persistent *quack*s
Female cackling
Rhaeb-rhaeb call
Grunt-whistle

12. Spotted Sandpiper
Weet and *peet-weet* calls
Rolling *peet-a-weet!* call
Rapid *weet*-series
Squeal call

13. Tree Swallow
Chideep call
Buzz call
Short song
Dawn song

14. Marsh Wren
Song
Buzz call
Chit alarm call
Churr call
Twitter song

15. Common Yellowthroat
Song
Flight song
Tschat & *steek!* alarm calls
Rapid chatter

16. Red-winged Blackbird
Song
Female sputter
Tsk! call
Male *seeeyer* alarm call
Twitter call

17. Barred Owl
Typical hoot-series
Whoo-ah
Ascending hoot-series
Greeting duet no. 1
Greeting duet no. 2
Immature screeches

FOREST AND PINE WOODS

18. Great Horned Owl
Typical hoot-series
Barklike alarm hoots
Screeches and bill-snapping

19. Downy Woodpecker
Pik call
Pik-series and subtle *churr*s
Whinny call
Harsh chatter
Drumming

20. Hairy Woodpecker
Peek call
Sputter call
Weeka-weeka and *tew-tew* calls
Drumming

21. Pileated Woodpecker
Short call
Cak-series
Gawaik-gawaik
Drumming

22. Great-crested Flycatcher
*Weeeps, prrrrrt!*s, and outbursts
Greeting duets
Dawn song

23. Eastern Wood-Pewee
Normal song
Dawn song
Turree call
Whines and sputters

24. Wood Thrush
Song
Wit volley (alarm)
Bub-bub-bub call
Zeee! call

25. Rose-breasted Grosbeak
Song
Chink call
Teeyoo fledgling call
Veee call

26. Scarlet Tanager
Song
Chick-bree call
Chip alarm call
Sweet call

NORTHWOODS AND HIGH MOUNTAINS

27. Yellow-bellied Sapsucker
Drumming
Mew call
Squeal-series
Grinding call and flight chatter

28. Hermit Thrush
Song
Churt alarm call
Wayyy call
Veee call

29. Dark-eyed Junco
Song
Tsip call
Tick alarm call

Zeeet and *titit!* calls
Fledgling *zeeet* call
Tew-tew call

30. Common Raven
Typical adult croaks
Immature harsh croak
Low *crok*
Unusual raven sounds

31. Common Loon
Tremolo call
Tremolo duet
Wail
Yodel
Hoot

SALT MARSH AND SEASHORE

32. Least Tern
*Chiddi*t call
Chiddy-what-it flight call
Chit alarm call
Zhreeek alarm call
Klee-series

33. Herring Gull
Klee-ew call
Plaintive *mew* call
Trumpeting call
Ga-ga-ga-ga alarm call
Hough-hough call

34. Clapper Rail
Kuk-kuk-kuk call
Grunt-series
Kicker call (*kick-kick-kick-kickerrrrrr*)

35. Willet
Day, day-deeyut, and *willillillet*
Kip and *keeer* alarm calls
Pill-will-willet courtship call